LIVING GREEN

ENERGY

Information and projects to reduce your environmental footprint

Marshall Cavendish
Benchmark
New York

Helen Whittaker

This edition first published in 2012 in the United States of America by
Marshall Cavendish Benchmark
An imprint of Marshall Cavendish Corporation

Website: www.marshallcavendish.us

This publication represents the opinions and views of the author based on Helen Whittaker's personal experience, knowledge, and research. The information in this book serves as a general guide only. The author and publisher have used their best efforts in preparing this book and disclaim liability rising directly and indirectly from the use and application of this book.

Other Marshall Cavendish Offices:
Marshall Cavendish Ltd. 5th Floor, 32-38 Saffron Hill, London EC1N 8FH, UK • Marshall Cavendish International (Asia) Private Limited, 1 New Industrial Road, Singapore 536196 • Marshall Cavendish International (Thailand) Co Ltd. 253 Asoke, 12th Flr, Sukhumvit 21 Road, Klongtoey Nua, Wattana, Bangkok 10110, Thailand • Marshall Cavendish (Malaysia) Sdn Bhd, Times Subang, Lot 46, Subang Hi-Tech Industrial Park, Batu Tiga, 40000 Shah Alam, Selangor Darul Ehsan, Malaysia

Marshall Cavendish is a trademark of Times Publishing Limited

All websites were available and accurate when this book was sent to press.

Library of Congress Cataloging-in-Publication Data

Whittaker, Helen, 1965–
    Energy / Helen Whittaker.
    p. cm. — (Living Green)
    Includes index.
    Summary: "Discusses how energy use impacts the environment and what you can do to be more eco-conscious"—Provided by publisher.
    ISBN 978-1-60870-573-3
    1. Energy conservation—Juvenile literature. 2. Power resources—Juvenile literature.
    I. Title.
    TJ163.35.W45 2012
    333.7916—dc22

                    2010044338

First published in 2011 by
MACMILLAN EDUCATION AUSTRALIA PTY LTD
15–19 Claremont Street, South Yarra 3141

Visit our website at www.macmillan.com.au or go directly to www.macmillanlibrary.com.au

Associated companies and representatives throughout the world.

Copyright © Macmillan Publishers Australia 2011

Publisher: Carmel Heron
Commissioning Editor: Niki Horin
Managing Editor: Vanessa Lanaway
Editor: Georgina Garner
Proofreader: Helena Newton
Designer: Julie Thompson
Page layout: Julie Thompson, Domenic Lauricella
Photo researcher: Claire Armstrong (management: Debbie Gallagher)
Illustrators: Alan Laver, Shelly Communications (**9, 10**);
Nives Porcellato and Andrew Craig (**12**); Cat MacInnes (all other illustrations)
Production Controller: Vanessa Johnson

Printed in China

Acknowledgments
The author and publisher are grateful to the following for permission to reproduce copyright material:

Front cover photograph: Boy looking out walkway courtesy of Getty Images/Silvestre Machado. Front and back cover illustrations by Cat MacInnes.

Photographs courtesy of: Corbis/Atlantide Phototravel, **13** (bottom), /Kevin Burke, **11** (bottom), /Hill Street Studios, **22**, /Ocean, **28**; Getty Images/ Tom Grill, **5**, /JupiterImages, **16**, /John Lund/Sam Diephuis, **19** (right), /Southern Stock, **26**; iStockphoto.com/Amilkin, **7** (bottom), /Ron Bailey, **7** (top), /Greg da Silva, **31**, /elgol, **17**, /RMAX, **15**; Photolibrary, **24**, /Alamy/Angela Hampton Picture Library, **20**; Shutterstock/abutyrin, **8** (bottom), / Akaiser, (environment icons, throughout), /Sinisa Botas, **19** (left), /Katrina Brown, **4, 32**, /Bryan Busovicki, **13** (top), /gsmad, **30** (middle), /Jeka, **14** (middle), /krivenko, **8** (top), /Laenz, (eco icons, throughout), /mmaxer, **30** (top), /Monkey Business Images, **3, 6, 14** (top), **18**, /Lobke Peers, **9** (top left), /Pixel1962, **9** (top right), /sepavo, **14** (bottom), /Smileus, **10**, /Brian Tan, **9** (bottom), /Zoran Vukmanov Simokov, **21**, /WDG Photo, **11** (top), / Ye, (recycle logos, throughout), /Jin Young Lee, **30** (bottom).

While every care has been taken to trace and acknowledge copyright, the publisher tenders their apologies for any accidental infringement where copyright has proved untraceable. They would be pleased to come to a suitable arrangement with the rightful owner in each case.

Please note
At the time of printing, the Internet addresses appearing in this book were correct. Owing to the dynamic nature of the Internet, however, we cannot guarantee that all these addresses will remain correct.

Contents

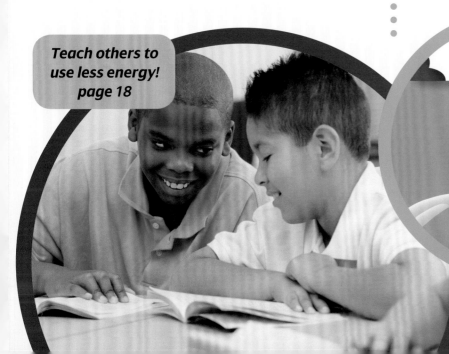

Teach others to use less energy! page 18

Use moving water to produce energy! page 28

Glossary Words

When a word is printed in **bold**, you can look up its meaning in the Glossary on page 31.

Living Green

Living green means choosing to care for the **environment** by living in a sustainable way.

Living Sustainably

Living sustainably means living in a way that protects Earth. Someone who lives sustainably avoids damaging the environment or wasting resources so that Earth can continue to provide a home for people in the future.

You and your friends can change your habits and behavior to help Earth. Living green makes sense!

How Our Actions Affect the Environment

Human activities use up Earth's **natural resources** and damage the environment. Some natural resources are **renewable**, such as wind and water, and some are **nonrenewable**, such as the **fossil fuels coal** and **oil**.

As the world's population grows, people are using more water, which creates water shortages, and are causing water **pollution**. We are using more nonrenewable resources too, which are usually mined from the earth and then burned, causing **habitat** destruction and air pollution. People cannot continue to live and act the way they do now—this way of life is unsustainable.

What Is an Environmental Footprint?

A person's environmental footprint describes how much damage that person does to the environment and how quickly the person uses up Earth's resources. A person who protects the environment and does not waste resources has a light environmental footprint. A person who pollutes the environment and wastes resources has a heavy environmental footprint.

Energy

We make an impact on the environment through the amount of energy we use and how this energy is **generated**. Understanding energy use can help us make greener choices and live more sustainably.

What Is Energy?

Energy is the ability to do work. Heat, light, motion, and electricity are examples of forms of energy. People have learned how to change one form of energy to another, for example by changing the energy stored in gasoline into motion. The things we get energy from are called energy sources.

How Energy Use Affects the Environment

The environmental effects of our energy use depend on the energy source and the way the energy is generated. Some energy sources are nonrenewable, such as oil, **natural gas**, coal, and **uranium**. Mining them can destroy habitats, and burning them to generate energy causes pollution, harms the environment, and uses up natural resources. Other energy sources such as the wind, water, and sun, are renewable and will not run out. Using these renewable energy sources has less environmental impact.

How Does Generating Electrical Energy from Coal Affect the Environment?

When you watch television, you use electrical energy. Some electricity is generated by burning coal. Generating this electricity can have many negative effects on the environment.

 Mining Coal

Coal is a fossil fuel. Mining coal uses up nonrenewable resources and destroys habitats.

 Transporting the Coal to a Power Plant

Trucks burn fossil fuels, which harms the environment and is not sustainable.

 Burning Coal to Generate Electricity

Burning coal releases **carbon dioxide**, which contributes to air pollution and **global warming**.

Where to Next?

• To find out how we use energy, where it comes from, and about sustainable forms of energy, go to the "Background Briefing" section on page 6.
• To try out fun projects that will help you reduce your environmental footprint, go to the "Living Green Projects" section on page 16.

How Do We Use Energy?

We use energy many times every day, for example when we take a shower, watch television, make a cup of hot chocolate, or surf the Internet. Generating this energy affects the environment.

Using Energy

We use energy at home and at school for lighting, heating, cooling, cooking, boiling water, and operating a wide range of electrical appliances. We also use energy to travel—from everyday journeys, such as taking the bus to school, to occasional journeys, such as flying somewhere for a vacation.

Electrical Appliances

A lot of the electrical energy we use every day is used to power electrical appliances. Different electrical appliances have different power ratings, which are measured in watts (w) or kilowatts (kw). One kilowatt hour (1 kwh) is the amount of energy that an appliance with a power of 1 kilowatt uses during one hour. The more energy an appliance uses, the greater its environmental impact.

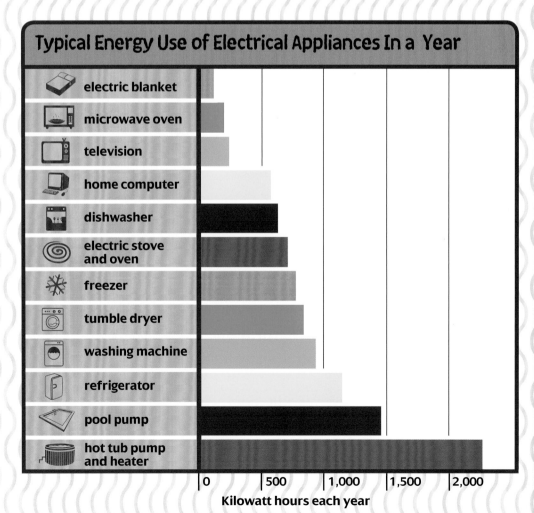

Typical Energy Use of Electrical Appliances In a Year

electric blanket
microwave oven
television
home computer
dishwasher
electric stove and oven
freezer
tumble dryer
washing machine
refrigerator
pool pump
hot tub pump and heater

0   500   1,000   1,500   2,000

Kilowatt hours each year

Batteries

Some appliances are powered by batteries. Batteries change stored chemical energy into electrical energy. Making disposable batteries uses up nonrenewable resources. When disposable batteries are thrown away, they become **landfill** and **toxic** chemicals leak out of them and pollute the environment. When rechargeable batteries run out, they are connected to an electrical charger, which restores the chemical energy so they can be used again and again.

Some of your toys get their energy from batteries. Rechargeable batteries are better for the environment than disposable batteries.

Using Energy Indirectly

When we think about our energy use, it is easy to overlook all the energy that we use indirectly, such as the energy that is used to grow, process, and transport the food we eat. Energy is also used to **manufacture** and transport the goods we buy.

ECO FACT

A 25-watt energy-saving lightbulb gives out about the same amount of light as a 100-watt **incandescent lightbulb**, but it uses less energy and lasts between eight and fifteen times longer. Some countries have banned the production of incandescent lightbulbs.

The different fruits in your supermarket could have come from many different places around the world. A lot of energy is used to transport these foods long distances.

Where Does Our Energy Come From?

The energy we use comes from a range of sources. Some of these are renewable, such as wind and water, and some are nonrenewable, such as coal and oil.

Nonrenewable Energy Sources

Most countries rely heavily on nonrenewable energy sources. Nonrenewable energy sources are unsustainable because they cannot be replaced.

How Much Energy Comes from Renewable Sources?

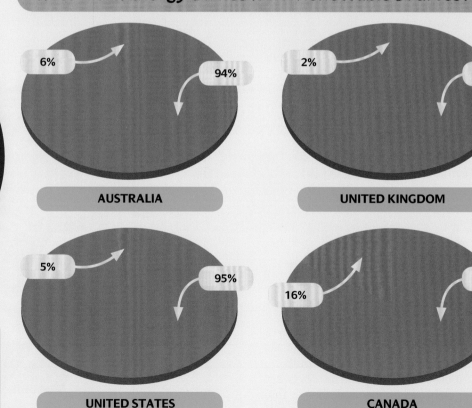

6%   94%

AUSTRALIA

2%   98%

UNITED KINGDOM

5%   95%

UNITED STATES

16%   84%

CANADA

KEY: ▮ Nonrenewable energy sources   ▮ Renewable energy sources

Like most countries, Australia, Canada, the United Kingdom, and the United States rely heavily on nonrenewable energy sources. This is unsustainable.

Fossil Fuels

Coal, natural gas, and oil are fossil fuels. The fossil fuel most often used to generate electricity is coal. Natural gas is used for cooking and heating. Oil is used to make gasoline.

Before they can be used, fossil fuels must be mined, transported, and stored. This uses energy, creates pollution, and destroys habitats.

Fossil fuels are burned to change their chemical energy into other forms of energy. When burned, they release harmful substances that pollute the air. These substances include carbon dioxide and other **greenhouse gases**, which contribute to global warming.

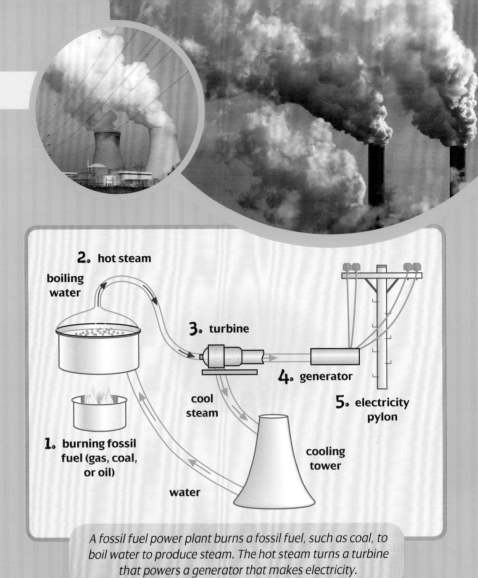

2. hot steam

boiling water

3. turbine

4. generator

cool steam

5. electricity pylon

1. burning fossil fuel (gas, coal, or oil)

cooling tower

water

A fossil fuel power plant burns a fossil fuel, such as coal, to boil water to produce steam. The hot steam turns a turbine that powers a generator that makes electricity.

Most cars run on gasoline, which comes from a nonrenewable energy source called oil. The world's oil supply will eventually run out.

9

Nuclear Energy

Nuclear energy is the energy in the nucleus, or core, of an atom. An atom is the smallest part of a substance. In nuclear power plants, the atoms of a **radioactive** substance called uranium are split apart. This nuclear reaction releases huge amounts of energy, which is used to make electricity. Uranium is a nonrenewable resource that is mined from the ground.

ECO FACT

On April 26, 1986, there was a fire at the Chernobyl nuclear power plant in Ukraine. More than four thousand people are eventually expected to die due to the radiation that was released during this fire.

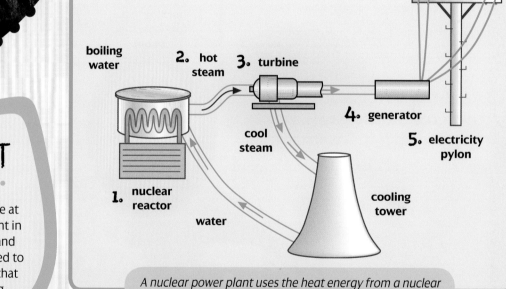

A nuclear power plant uses the heat energy from a nuclear reaction to boil water to produce steam. The steam turns a turbine that powers a generator that makes electricity.

Advantages and Disadvantages of Nuclear Energy

Advantages	Disadvantages
✔ Nuclear power plants are very **energy efficient.** They convert a large amount of the fuel's energy into electricity.	✖ Radioactive waste is dangerous and must be stored safely.
✔ Nuclear energy does not produce much air pollution.	✖ If there is an accident, **radiation** may leak into the environment, killing or harming living things.

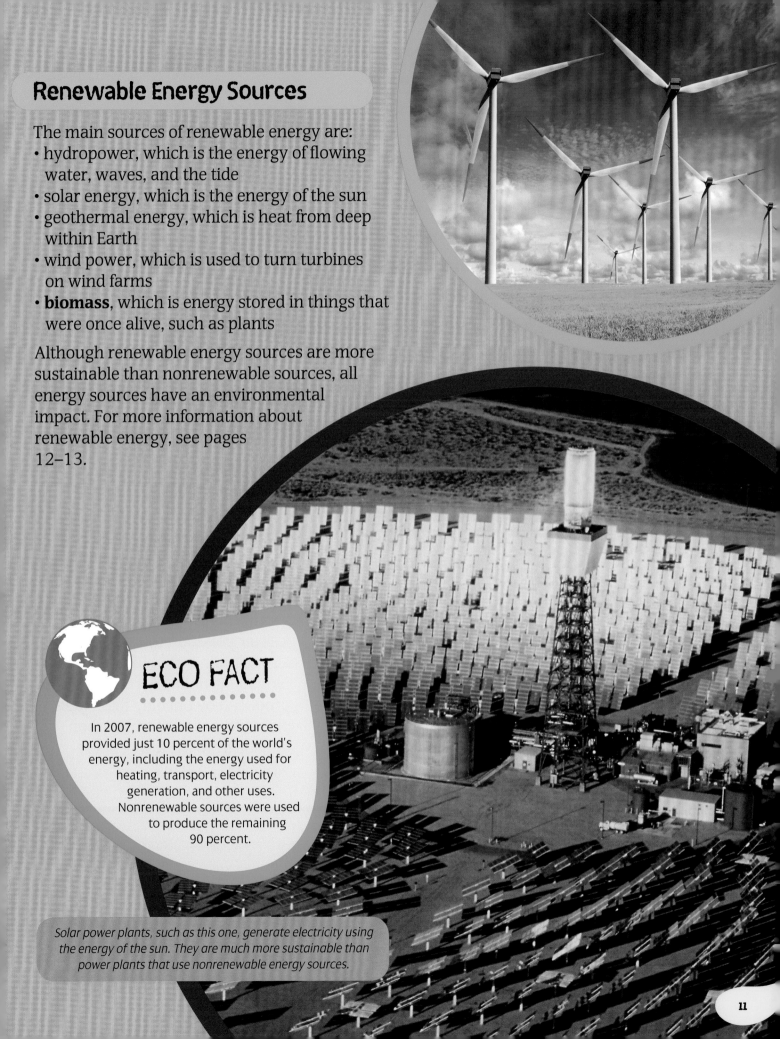

Renewable Energy Sources

The main sources of renewable energy are:
- hydropower, which is the energy of flowing water, waves, and the tide
- solar energy, which is the energy of the sun
- geothermal energy, which is heat from deep within Earth
- wind power, which is used to turn turbines on wind farms
- **biomass**, which is energy stored in things that were once alive, such as plants

Although renewable energy sources are more sustainable than nonrenewable sources, all energy sources have an environmental impact. For more information about renewable energy, see pages 12–13.

ECO FACT

In 2007, renewable energy sources provided just 10 percent of the world's energy, including the energy used for heating, transport, electricity generation, and other uses. Nonrenewable sources were used to produce the remaining 90 percent.

Solar power plants, such as this one, generate electricity using the energy of the sun. They are much more sustainable than power plants that use nonrenewable energy sources.

11

Are Renewable Energy Sources Green?

Renewable energy sources will not run out, so they are more sustainable than nonrenewable resources such as fossil fuels and uranium. But generating energy from renewable sources still has environmental impacts.

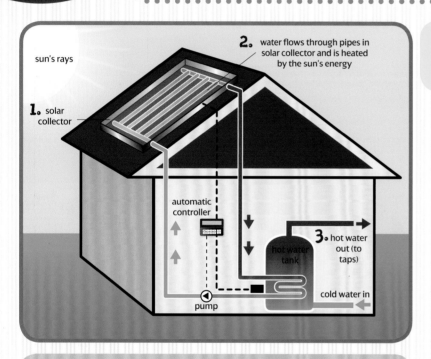

sun's rays

2. water flows through pipes in solar collector and is heated by the sun's energy

1. solar collector

automatic controller

hot water tank

3. hot water out (to taps)

cold water in

pump

A solar collector captures heat from the sun and uses it to heat water. It does this without burning any fuel and without causing any air pollution.

The Advantages of Renewable Energy

Renewable energy sources are more sustainable than nonrenewable energy sources because:
- renewable resources will never run out
- solar energy, wind, and hydropower do not produce air pollution
- geothermal energy produces a lot less air pollution than fossil fuels
- air pollution from burning biomass is not as harmful as that produced by burning fossil fuels
- plant biomass absorbs carbon dioxide from the atmosphere while it is growing

World Renewable Energy Production

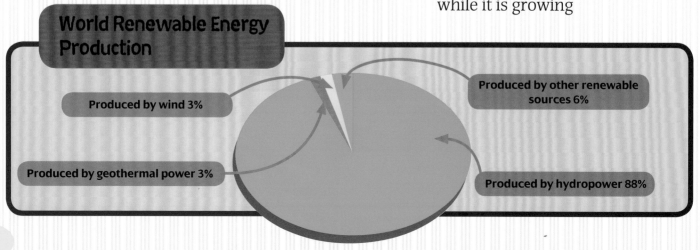

Produced by wind 3%

Produced by other renewable sources 6%

Produced by geothermal power 3%

Produced by hydropower 88%

The Environmental Impact of Renewable Energy Sources

Even though renewable energy sources are more sustainable than nonrenewable sources, they still have an environmental impact.

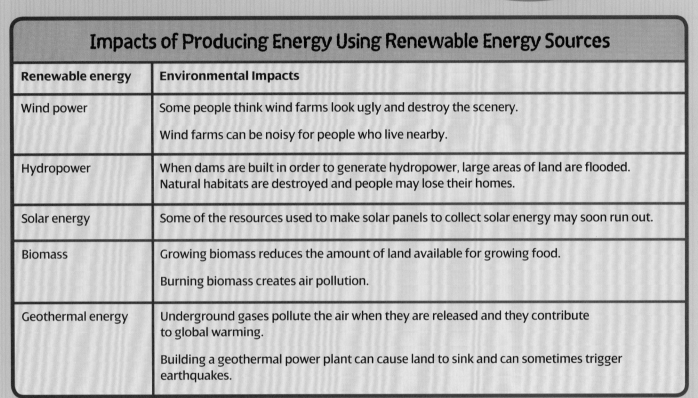

Impacts of Producing Energy Using Renewable Energy Sources	
Renewable energy	**Environmental Impacts**
Wind power	Some people think wind farms look ugly and destroy the scenery. Wind farms can be noisy for people who live nearby.
Hydropower	When dams are built in order to generate hydropower, large areas of land are flooded. Natural habitats are destroyed and people may lose their homes.
Solar energy	Some of the resources used to make solar panels to collect solar energy may soon run out.
Biomass	Growing biomass reduces the amount of land available for growing food. Burning biomass creates air pollution.
Geothermal energy	Underground gases pollute the air when they are released and they contribute to global warming. Building a geothermal power plant can cause land to sink and can sometimes trigger earthquakes.

ECO FACT

Iceland produces all of its electricity from renewable sources. About 70 percent is produced by hydropower and 30 percent by geothermal power.

Bathers enjoy the warm water in a lake beside one of Iceland's many geothermal power plants. These power plants use very hot water from beneath the ground to turn turbines and generate electricity. The plants then use the water for hot water systems and also to fill lakes for people to swim and play in.

What Can You Do?

There are many ways that you can use energy more sustainably. The best way is simply to use less energy! This is easy to do and it will reduce the impact you have on the environment.

Green Tips to Use Less Energy Directly

Here are some easy ways to start saving energy.

✔ Ask your parents or the principal of your school to replace incandescent lightbulbs with energy-saving lightbulbs.

✔ Turn off appliances when they are not in use, instead of leaving them run on standby.

✔ Instead of turning on the heat when you are cold, put on extra clothes.

✔ Instead of turning on the air-conditioning when you are hot, have a cold drink to cool down.

✔ Walk or bicycle to school instead of taking the bus or car.

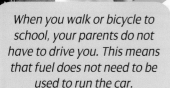

When you walk or bicycle to school, your parents do not have to drive you. This means that fuel does not need to be used to run the car.

Green Tips to Use Less Energy

If you start thinking about the types of food you eat and the types of goods you buy, you can begin to reduce the amount of energy that you use. Energy is used to make all manufactured goods, and it takes a lot of energy to transport food and goods long distances.

✔ Choose more locally grown food or grow some of your own food.

✔ Buy more goods that are made locally from local materials.

✔ Fix broken things rather than replacing them.

✔ When you buy new goods, choose well-made items that will last a long time.

You can buy locally made goods at local craft markets. These goods have often used less energy than goods that have been transported long distances.

Living Green Ratings and Green Tips

Pages 16–29 are filled with fun projects that will help you understand how and when you use energy and how you can save energy.

Each project is given its own Living Green star rating—from zero to five—as a measurement of how much the project lightens your environmental footprint.

Some projects give Green Tips telling you how you can improve the project's Living Green rating even more.

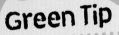

Green Tip

To improve the Living Green rating, make the strap from an old belt or a bicycle inner tube.

On each project spread, look for the Living Green rating. Five stars is the highest—and greenest—rating!

Living Green Rating
★★★★★

★★★	★★★★	★★★★★
A three-star project will teach you about an issue and explain how you are wasting natural resources or causing pollution.	A four-star project will show one or two ways to reduce garbage or pollution.	A five-star project will help you reduce garbage and pollution and actively protect the environment in many different ways.

How Energy Efficient Is Your Home or School?

What You Need

• Pencil
• Paper

Take a survey and compare your results with friends

Take this short survey to find out how energy efficient your home or school is. An energy-efficient building is one in which very little energy is wasted.

What to Do

1. Decide whether you will do the survey about your home or your school.

2. Read the questions in the survey. On a piece of paper, write down your answers as A, B, or C.

3. Score yourself three points for every A, two points for every B, and one point for every C.

4. Add up your total and check your energy-efficiency rating, below.

5. Ask a teacher to make photocopies of page 17 and get your friends to try the survey too. Compare your results. Who has the most energy-efficient home or school?

Energy-Efficiency Rating

7–10 points:	Poor
11–14 points:	Average
15–18 points:	Good
19–21 points:	Excellent

Using energy-saving lightbulbs can make your home or school more energy efficient.

SURVEY QUESTIONS

1. How many lightbulbs in your home or school are energy-saving?

    A. All of them   B. Some of them   C. None of them

2. Are electrical appliances such as computers and televisions left on standby?

    A. Never   B. Sometimes   C. Always

3. Is your home or school **insulated**? Ask your parents or school principal.

    A. Fully   B. Partly   C. No

4. Are the windows in your home or school double glazed (do they have two sheets of glass with space between them)? Ask your parents or school principal.

    A. Fully   B. Partly   C. No

5. How is your home or school heated?

    A. Solar heating or geothermal heat pump
    B. Wood burner, heat pump, or heating below the floor   C. Other

6. How is the water heated?

    A. Solar energy or wood burner   B. Gas   C. Other

7. How often is the air conditioner on?

    A. We don't use an air-conditioner   B. Sometimes in the summer
    C. Most of the time in the summer

Green Tip

In the summer, close curtains to block out heat and keep your house or school cool. In the winter, open your curtains to let in the warm morning sun. This will help you save energy that would normally be used to cool or heat your home or school.

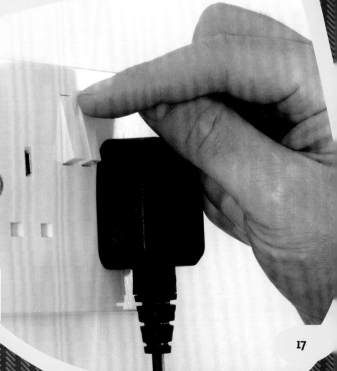

Switching appliances off at the outlet can make your home and school more energy efficient.

Saving Energy at School

Get your whole school "living green"

Sometimes it's hard to see all the ways that we use energy. Organize a day to educate other students about energy use and to find ways of using less energy at school.

Living Green Rating

★ ★ ★ ★ ★

- Raises awareness of how much energy your school uses
- Encourages other students and teachers to save energy, which reduces the need to burn fossil fuels to generate energy, so the environmental impact is smaller

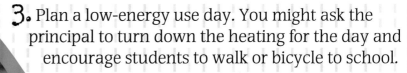

What to Do

1. Ask your teacher or principal if your class can organize a low-energy-use day at school.

2. Take the survey on page 17 to find out how energy efficient your school is. Think about where energy efficiency can be improved.

3. Plan a low-energy use day. You might ask the principal to turn down the heating for the day and encourage students to walk or bicycle to school.

4. Tell your teacher or principal your plan, and see if they have any suggestions.

5. Organize your class into three groups.

6. One group could make and put up posters about the event. The posters could give tips about saving energy on that day. See the tips on page 19 for some ideas.

7. One group could talk to younger classes and explain what energy is, how we use it, where it comes from, and why it is important to use less of it.

8. The last group could make reminder signs for the day, such as "When you're finished, turn it off" signs for computer monitors.

Explain to other students why it is important to use less energy. You can teach them about living green!

Drawing the blinds on hot days keeps the heat out and you won't need to use air conditioning. Each time you do this, you are helping to save Earth.

Green Tips to Save Energy at School

* Set the heating **thermostat** a few degrees cooler.

* Set the air-conditioning thermostat a few degrees warmer.

* Put on an extra layer of clothing instead of turning on the heat.

* Draw the curtains on hot days instead of turning on the air-conditioner.

* Replace incandescent lightbulbs with energy-saving lightbulbs.

* Switch off electrical appliances rather than leaving them on standby.

* Switch off lights when no one is in the room.

Styrofoam Insulation

See how insulation affects energy use

Insulation keeps a building cooler in the summer and warmer in the winter. It's a clever way to reduce the amount of energy needed for cooling and heating. Try this experiment to see how insulation traps heat inside a building.

Living Green Rating

★ ★ ★

- Shows you how insulation can save energy, which reduces the need to burn fossil fuels to generate energy, making the environmental impact smaller

What You Need

- Shoebox
- Scissors
- Adhesive tape
- Styrofoam
- Lightbulb holder with cable and plug
- Incandescent lightbulb
- Timer
- Thermometer
- Pencil
- Paper

What to Do

1. Use the scissors to make a small hole in one end of the box. Poke the thermometer through, with the bulb end inside the box.

2. Make another hole at the other end of the box and fix the lightbulb holder in it.

3. Put the lightbulb in the holder.

In this experiment, the temperature inside your shoebox works like the temperature inside a heated room or building.

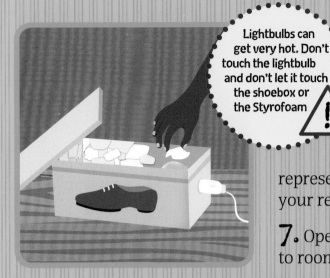

4. Put the lid on the box.

5. Switch the lightbulb on for fifteen minutes.

6. Switch off the lightbulb. Write down temperature readings every five minutes for the next thirty minutes. This part of the experiment represents a heated building without any insulation. Label your results "No insulation."

7. Open the lid of the box and let the air inside get back to room temperature. Allow at least twenty minutes.

8. Stick Styrofoam to all the inside surfaces of the box, including the underside of the lid.

9. Repeat steps four to six. This part of the experiment represents a heated building with insulation in its roof, walls, and floor. Label these results "Has insulation."

What You Will Discover

When the box is insulated, the air inside cools down more slowly. In an insulated building, less heat is lost to the outside so less energy is needed to keep it heated.

Green Tip

Styrofoam is used to make some coffee cups and some pellets for packing. Wash out old Styrofoam cups, dry them, and use them in this experiment.

Lightbulb versus Lightbulb

Test the energy efficiency of two types of lightbulbs

Some lightbulbs waste energy because they lose a lot of their energy in the form of heat. Try this experiment to compare the heat given off by incandescent lightbulbs and energy-saving lightbulbs.

What You Need

- Gooseneck lamp
- 100-watt incandescent lightbulb
- 25-watt energy-saving lightbulb
- Thermometer
- Ruler
- White towel
- Timer
- Paper
- Pencil

What to Do

1. Lay the towel flat on a table.

2. Place the thermometer at one end of the towel.

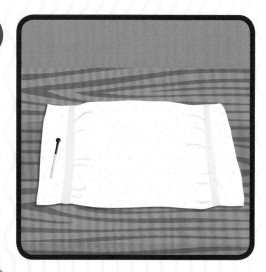

3. Make sure the lamp is unplugged. Screw the incandescent lightbulb into the lamp.

4. Position the head of the lamp so that the lightbulb is close to the thermometer.

One of these lightbulbs wastes more energy. Which one is it?

5. Measure the distance between the lightbulb and the thermometer and make a note of it.

6. Plug in and switch on the lamp. Leave it on for ten minutes.

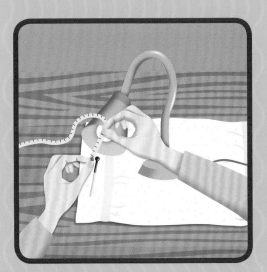

7. Record the temperature on the thermometer.

8. Switch off the lamp. Allow everything to cool down for at least twenty minutes.

9. Unplug the lamp. Remove the incandescent lightbulb and replace it with the other lightbulb.

10. Place the head of the lamp so that the lightbulb is close to the thermometer. Make sure the distance between the two is the same as it was before.

11. Repeat steps six to eight.

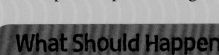

What Should Happen

The thermometer should give a higher reading underneath the incandescent lightbulb. This is because incandescent lightbulbs lose a lot of energy as heat. Energy-saving lightbulbs produce less heat so they are more energy efficient.

From Scraps to Methane

Find out how to get energy from garbage

When plant and animal waste rot, they don't just smell terrible — they also release a **flammable** gas called **methane**. Gas produced in this way is called biogas, and it can be used for cooking or heating.

What You Need

- One-third cup mixture of vegetable scraps and grass
- One-third cup soil
- Mixing bowl
- Spoon
- Funnel
- 0.25-gallon (1-liter) plastic bottle
- Balloon
- Duct tape
- Permanent marker
- String
- Ruler
- Paper
- Pencil

What to Do

1. Thoroughly mix together the vegetable scraps, grass, and soil.

2. Using the funnel, pour the mixture into the bottle.

3. Stretch the neck of the balloon over the top of the bottle. Seal with duct tape.

Vegetable scraps are a type of plant waste. Use your scraps to create methane gas.

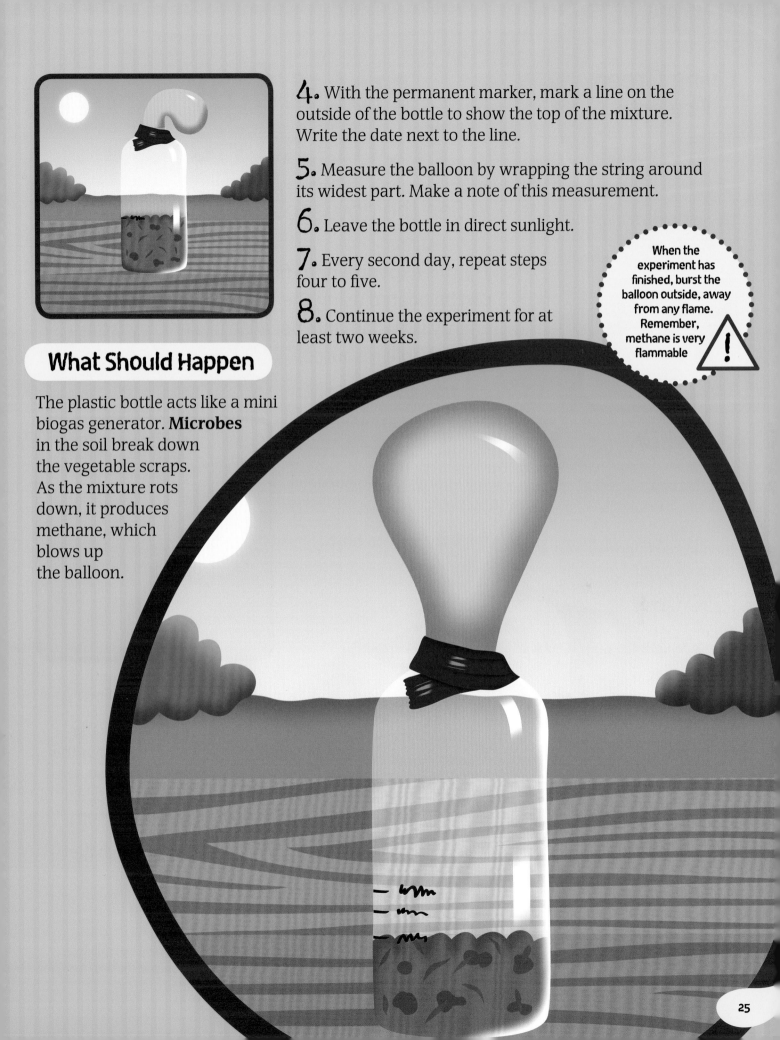

4. With the permanent marker, mark a line on the outside of the bottle to show the top of the mixture. Write the date next to the line.

5. Measure the balloon by wrapping the string around its widest part. Make a note of this measurement.

6. Leave the bottle in direct sunlight.

7. Every second day, repeat steps four to five.

8. Continue the experiment for at least two weeks.

When the experiment has finished, burst the balloon outside, away from any flame. Remember, methane is very flammable ⚠

What Should Happen

The plastic bottle acts like a mini biogas generator. **Microbes** in the soil break down the vegetable scraps. As the mixture rots down, it produces methane, which blows up the balloon.

Hot Water From the Hose

See the power of the sun's energy

Try this experiment to find out how easily water can be heated using the power of the sun. Solar energy is sustainable because it is energy from a renewable resource.

Living Green Rating

★ ★ ★ ★

- Demonstrates how you can use solar energy instead of electricity, which reduces the need to burn fossil fuels to generate electricity, making the environmental impact smaller

What You Need

- Outside tap
- Garden hose with a nozzle
- Bucket
- Black duct tape
- Scissors

What to Do

1. On a sunny day, go outside around noon.

2. Attach the garden hose to the outside tap.

3. Turn the tap on gently.

4. As soon as water starts coming out the end of the hose, twist the hose nozzle until the water stops.

5. Switch the tap off.

You can heat your own water using just a garden hose and the sun.

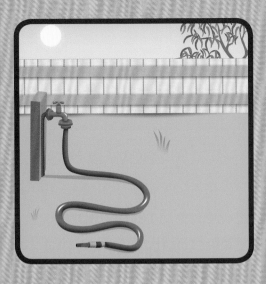

6. Lay the hose in direct sunlight.

7. Come back in two to three hours.

8. Open the nozzle on the end of the hose and release the water into a bucket.

9. Cover the hose in black duct tape and repeat steps three to eight.

Be careful. The water inside the hose can get very hot

What Should Happen

The water that comes out of the hose should be hot. Black absorbs more energy than other colors, so if you cover the hose in black duct tape, it will absorb more of the sun's heat, and the water inside will get even hotter.

Green Tip

Don't throw away the hot water. Use it to wash your dog, do the dishes, or soak your dirty feet!

Make a Model Water Turbine

Witness the energy released by moving water

Water turbines use moving water, a renewable energy source, to generate electricity. Make your own model water turbine and see the amount of energy produced by flowing water.

Living Green Rating

★ ★ ★ ★

• Shows you how you can use moving water to generate energy, which would reduce the need to burn fossil fuels to generate energy, making the environmental impact smaller

What You Need

- 0.25-gallon (1-liter) empty milk or juice carton
- Nail
- String
- Masking tape
- Scissors
- Pitcher of water

What to Do

1. Use the nail to make a hole through the middle of the top part of the carton.

2. Push the string through the hole and tie it securely.

3. Make a hole in the bottom right-hand corner of each of the four faces of the carton.

4. Tape up each hole with masking tape.

Ask an adult to help you make the holes with a nail ⚠️

Fill up a pitcher from the tap and get ready to power your own water turbine!

5. Hang the carton somewhere where it can hang freely and where it doesn't matter if you spill water. Fill it with water.

6. Pull off the tape from one corner. Watch what happens.

7. Pull off the tape from the opposite corner. Watch what happens.

8. Pull off the tape from the remaining two corners. Watch what happens.

What Should Happen

The water will pour out of the holes and the force will push the carton in the opposite direction. The carton will begin to spin. The more holes that are open, the faster the carton will spin.

Green Tip

Perform this experiment over a dry lawn or garden bed, so that the water is not wasted.

Find Out More About Living Green

The Internet is a great way of finding out more about how energy generation affects the environment and uses natural resources. You can also find out how to save energy and make more sustainable energy choices.

Useful Websites

Visit these useful websites:

www.eere.energy.gov/kids
This website features tips for saving energy and some fun energy-saving games.

http://tonto.eia.doe.gov/kids/index.cfm
This website gives lots of information about energy use and generation, and how to save energy.

http://unep.org/tunza/children
This website from the United Nations has downloadable fact sheets about environmental issues, tips for living more sustainably, and competitions you can enter.

Searching for Information

Here are some terms you might enter into your Internet search bar to find out more about energy and the environment:
- renewable energy
- fossil fuels
- energy efficiency
- global warming

Glossary

biomass Plant matter that can be burned to produce energy.

carbon dioxide A greenhouse gas that is released when fossil fuels are burned, for example when coal is burned to make electricity.

coal A type of rock that formed from the remains of plants that lived hundreds of millions of years ago.

energy efficient Using a small amount of energy compared to other similar items.

environment The natural world, including plants, animals, land, rivers, and oceans.

flammable Easily set on fire.

fossil fuels Coal, oil, and natural gas, which are natural resources that are formed from remains of dead plants and animals, deep under Earth's surface, over millions of years.

generated Produced energy that can be used by changing it from one form, such as chemical energy, to another form, such as electrical energy.

global warming The process by which Earth's average temperature is getting warmer.

greenhouse gases Gases, such as carbon dioxide or water vapor, that trap the heat of the sun in Earth's atmosphere.

habitat Place where plants and animals live.

incandescent lightbulb Common, pear-shaped lightbulb that produces light by heating a thin, coiled wire until it glows white-hot.

insulated Layered with material to stop heat from escaping and heat from entering.

landfill Garbage that is buried and covered with soil at garbage dumps.

manufacture Make from raw materials into a product for people to buy and use.

methane A type of greenhouse gas that is the main part of both natural gas and biogas.

microbes Tiny living things, most of which are too small to be seen with the naked eye; microbes include bacteria and fungi.

natural gas A gas found underground, often with other fossil fuels such as coal and oil; it is mainly made up of methane.

natural resources Natural materials that can be used by people, such as wood, metal, coal, and water.

nonrenewable resources Natural resources that cannot be easily replaced, such as coal, oil, and natural gas.

oil A liquid found in rocks, formed from the remains of plants and animals that lived millions of years ago.

pollution Damaging substances, especially chemicals or waste products, that harm the environment.

radiation A form of energy, also called ionizing radiation, that is harmful to living things.

radioactive Releasing energy in the form of ionizing radiation, which is harmful to living things.

renewable resources Natural resources that will never run out, such as the wind, or that can easily be replaced, such as wood.

thermostat Device for controlling the temperature of a heating or cooling system.

toxic Poisonous to living things.

uranium A silvery-white, radioactive metal that is the main fuel used in nuclear power stations.

Index